NevaEva

MW00397276

Why we're broke and they're rich!

Author: Isaiah Donaldson Jr.

Book Series:
Re-educating the culture

Introduction

Power comes with respect. Money comes with power. Time never stops. It just continues to move. Change happens, but only in time. Nothing changes without the proper conditions for evolution.

My people expect change, but aren't willing to work for it. Change is necessary when a group of people have been accustomed to a lifestyle which is the result of laziness and failure.

No one fails a task that they have not attempted to achieve. No one achieves a task that they have not attempted to achieve.

Therefore, my people will never succeed in a life that they are not willing to work hard for. You see. The difference between my people and their people is the work ethic.

The work ethic plays a big part in the success of not just one, but all. All of them show great work ethic. All of my people don't. All of their people succeed due to their knowledge about the lifestyle that they have chosen to live.

None of my people have that same knowledge. We lack the knowledge that they share amongst each other behind closed doors. While they pass along the tools to fix their life to be a certain way, we pass along our tools to fix our lives to be our way and guess who we pass it to?

Our friends, our family and the saddest thing about this awful lifestyle is that we teach it to our children!

The ones that we are supposed to teach how to succeed, we teach how to fail. I'm ready for a change. I'm ready to improve over time.

My people speak of the phenomenon called advancement without the correct understanding of it. We need to learn. We need to teach. We need to overcome!

How long will we fail before we acknowledge our failure! We've failed in our achievements. We failed in our belief system. We've also failed to advance and change with time.

Today we win! Today we learn how to win! Today will show us the ways of tomorrow. Evolution happens right now!

No longer will we be the laughing stock of the world. No longer will we teach our children to be poor. Why should we? Why do we?

When enough is enough we will be able to explain why? Do you know what we will be able to say? It's our time to live a great lifestyle because we have worked hard for it.

We made it happen and we will teach our children how to continue. We as a people have to improve our teaching skills. As a whole we are at the bottom. So, as a whole we have to rise and explain how to rise, but before we can overcome our situation.

We must be honest with ourselves. We can't keep acting as if our bad habits are good. As of right now we have to come together and learn our true problem. This is "why we're broke and they're rich."

Index:
Chapter 1-What is "Broke"
Chapter 2-Self awareness
Chapter 3-What's our problem
Chapter 4- How do we correct our problem
Chapter 5- What is support
Chapter 6-Stop being content
Chapter 7- What "they" know
Chapter 8- The uprising of lower class

Chapter 1
What is "Broke"

Since the beginning of time, there has been a psychological separation between certain types of people. Mentally all have the same capability, but not everyone uses it the same.

There are people that think small. There are people that think big. When a person is stronger than another psychologically it will show. You can clearly see the difference between the human that wants to eat plants and the human who is hungry for meat.

They are not satisfied with the same foods. One can live in a small garden and feel good. The other will mentally feel as though they are not living to their full potential.

This will force them to strive for more. In this sense they would not feel comfortable until they live on a farm where they can eat meat.

Once both people live according to their own morals and values, they will feel successful. This is what makes a person happy. Living in fulfillment of their morals and values.

In the 21st century the morals and values of every nation has been chosen for them. Who chose them for each nation? That is a topic that goes beyond this book.

There are millions of theories on "how" but that is not the purpose of this discussion. What we need to identify is, what place do we fall in this "structure," that was set for us in this nation.

In the twenty-first century there has been a structure that was obviously set for us. What we know today is that this structure starts with a few at the top. Then it grows as it goes to the bottom.

The further you are from the top of this structure, the more people you find like you. There are way more people at the very bottom than at the very top. It's like a pyramid.

The bottom is very wide and is the bigger part. It's the foundation of the entire body. As you go up, it begins to get smaller. All the way until it gets to the little point at the top.

This is the image of our human structure that we live in. The bottom of the human structure makes the top stand up! The bottom of the human structure holds up the entire pyramid.

Without the bottom there would and could be no top! Now, the entire human race has to accept their positions in the human structure in order for it to remain the way it is.

The top must want to stay at the top. They must accept their role in the human race as the leaders or rulers. Without them playing their role correctly, it could mess up the entire structure.

If they make the wrong move and allow anyone to rise to their level of power. It could create a domino effect. It could also be the ultimate reason for the destruction of that human structure that has already been created.

Everyone in this structure must accept their role in order for the top to remain at the top and the bottom to remain at the bottom. No one has to truly agree with it, but everyone has to participate in it.

" Continue to play your role in the pyramid structure of the human race." This is what they say. For many years the structure has remained the same. With the same group of people at the top and the same groups of people at the bottom.

Sad to say but the human structure has been the same for thousands of years. The same people that have been in power of the structure make sure time after time that their pyramid does not be altered.

Hundreds and hundreds of years have passed, but there has been no difference in the layout of the pyramids. Once people die, their position is just given to their children in order to keep it going in the same order.

The top keeps their power that way. It stays in the family. I mean why would anyone with power over everything give it to anyone other than their children? Why would they allow someone else to control their family?

It would be crazy of them! Now this might be shocking for some people. If you know the truth about " history" then you should know the truth about the human structure.

It has been controlled by the same people for centuries. History and religion both speak about the structure. They all give credit to the Roman empire for becoming the final leaders of the human structure!

Thousands of years ago the Roman empire took control of the structure and has not lost their power since. They are the "top of the food chain." Years of domination have come from the Roman empire. No one has been able to stop them.

The top of the human structure consists of their Pope and their royal families. They rule the world as far as we know. When the Roman empire took over the structure, they gave power to the people that they knew.

They have given out an order of things. Why? To make sure that they remain at the top. Centuries after they have taken over the structure and it has been preciously altered for that reason.

For many hundreds of years slaves were at the very bottom of the structure! They were the ones that worked for nothing so that the rulers could gain everything. Slaves grew all of the crops. Slaves did all of the labor. Slaves did all of the work, while the Masters received all of the benefits!

Think about it. Honestly! How hard is it to become very rich when you have thousands of people working for you for free? You have no wages to pay your employees!

Slaves were at the very bottom of the human structure. It gets no lower than a slave in any society. Their masters were above them in the structure, but they were not at the top.

Oh no! They were definitely not at the top. They still had people that they had to answer to.

History check!

There were people that they had to ask for permission to even partake in the slave trade. For decades slaves were taken from country to country. Island to island. State to state.

In order to increase the chances of remaining at the top of the human civilization they had to increase the number at the bottom! This increase happened for years, even after slavery started.

The removal of civilized people from their natural state made it very easy to keep them from understanding the truth about themselves. Power was given to various people in direct cahoots with the Roman empire.

The very tip top of the pyramid has passed down a certain order for everyone beneath them. All the way to the foundation. Fast forward to today. The beautiful 21st century. The structure for most countries are the same in many ways.

Here in America it has been the same since 1619 when this country was founded. The rulers may have been altered for the appearance of time, but it is still the exact same structure.

Think about it. I mean why would anyone with power over everything give it to anyone other than their children? Why would they allow someone else to control their family? When people die their position is just given to their children so that they could simply keep it going in the same order! Think about what position your family has held in the human structure of America since 1619. This is "why we're broke and they're rich!"

Chapter 2
SELF-AWARENESS

The ultimate inspiration comes from self-awareness. No one can be more than what they are, until their true self is recognized. Perseverance comes with preparation.

Now are you prepared to hear the truth?

You are a survivor! A survivor is someone who stands the seconds, minutes, hours, days, weeks, months, and years of the world. In the English language it is pronounced time.

Every second that passes by there is a change in the world. No matter what changes occur there are beings that remain beings, through those times of change. They are what you call survivors.

If there's a hurricane today, tornado tomorrow, and a terrorist attack next week in the city of one's residents. Any resident who makes it out of those harsh chain of events either injured or not. That is a survivor.

Survivors have a story that should be heard. Why? Because they stood through the changes of time. The generations after them need to hear their stories. Why, because they are the generations of survivors, which also makes them survivors.

9/11 was a tragic event in America which has changed this country forever. Many lives were taken. The stories of which can only be told by those lives that survived. Pearl harbor was it. devastating time in the history of this place called America. But no one knows the disaster like the survivors. As the generations after the survivors.

You are survivors and your family's story is important in what is classified as "history." The most destructive disaster on the earth was slavery! Slavery was the crew act of hatred done to people for hundreds of years consecutively.

People were beaten, raped, kidnapped, humiliated, and killed for the benefit of another group of people. People of which were the same skin color as yourself. They had the same hair texture, facial structure, and share the same family as you.

Millions were killed, but those who weren't killed became survivors! Without those beautiful survivors, there would be no beautiful children left of those people. Those children deserve a certain type of respect.

Only a strong human being can stand through such a hard time like slavery. The survivors of survivors need to know and teach about their struggles. Through every change in the world their are survivors, but there are none more important in the history of the world than those whom have survived slavery.

The beautiful brown skin people, light skin people all over the world deserve to be treated with honor because they have stood through time. The worst time known to mankind!

As a survivor you are to be proud of who you are because you are strong. To be a black human being in the 21st century, means your family has survived the brutal hundreds of years of humiliation, torture, and hatred that at one time was more common than love. Even happiness.

Don't take for granted who you are. At one time your family couldn't read, write, go to school, have fun, buy houses, own businesses, or even enjoy life as it should be enjoyed. Your family was not stupid or lazy. They were the victims of invasion and slavery.

Your family doesn't want you to forget the struggles of time, but they do want you to be wise and understand that you are beautiful. You are an intelligent African survivor!

Now with that being said. What will you do to separate yourself from that bad stigma that has been passed on to your family? I'm not speaking of racist acts!

I'm not trying to create hatred between people. I'm merely trying to get you to understand" why we're broke and they're rich."

Your family. Our family didn't own businesses or land to pass down to their children. They didn't have the correct education about finances to teach their family about financial stability.

They only knew what was taught to them. How to work for nothing! A mom can't teach her child something that she doesn't know. How could she? I need for you to understand that what is "broken" needs to be fixed.

Until it is fixed it will always be broken! Now, if a mom works her entire life for free. What will she have to leave her children when she dies? She has nothing! So in return she leaves nothing!

This will automatically make things harder for her children. She was broke and uneducated. So she left her children in the world broke and uneducated. Now her children will do what they know and continue the same broken mentality that she has passed down.

No disrespect to anyone, but how can a slave teach you how to be the president! That is not a subject that was taught to slaves! Remember " perseverance comes with preparation."

In order for a person to succeed and have a life of wealth. They have to be aware of what wealth is. The reason why we are still down is because we were never taught how to come up!

We've all watched our community struggle as a whole. We've seen our parents work for nothing our whole life. I mean of course nowadays we do get paid for our labor. Thank God, but it's truly not enough to have anything.

Don't get me wrong! It pays the bills. It gets those nice clothes and cars, but later on once we bought those things all we have left are those things! For so long as a people, as a community we haven't had anything. We couldn't.

So now that we have a chance to get something. Of course we are going to get what we know we've been missing. Nice shoes, nice clothes, and a big house.

For hundreds of years we were not allowed to have them, so now we are just taking advantage of this time. Which is not wrong. Everyone needs clothing. Everyone needs a place to rest and feel comfortable, but when it comes to " why we're broke and they're rich." We have to look at what we are doing that is keeping us broke.

Are we doing the same thing that the people before us did? Are we working for nothing? Back then they didn't get paid at all. They just worked for their masters and they received little benefits.

They had a place to sleep. Their masters made sure that they had a place to rest. So that they were able to work another day. They received food. If a slave didn't eat, they would have no energy to work.

It would also die! So as a master of such an operation like slavery that had to be smart enough to understand that you have to keep your slaves well rested and fed. They made sure that they had what they needed to continue their job.

Nothing more. In order to keep someone or a group of people at the bottom. You have to control their wants and needs. If they want more, they'll ask for more. If they know that they need more. They'll demand it!

When you want people to stay at the bottom. You have to establish needs and wants for them. "What do you need? Food. A place to live. What do you need? Some clothes. That's it.

They knew what your family needed. They knew what they wanted. They are the same ones that deprived them of everything and listened to what they begged for.

So when it was time to let them free, they knew what they needed! Think about it. If people have been slaves they're entire lives. They lived for free on their master's plantation. Right? They worked on their Master's plantation for free. Right?

They ate on their master's plantation for free. Right? Okay. So when they become free from slavery what do they take with them? What do they eat? Where will they live?

Obviously they don't get a retirement check! They never had a 401K plan! So what do they do?

They work for what they now lack. They work for what they used to receive for free! They work just to pay for food! Housing! Clothing! This is the only thing that they know. The things that they no longer have are the only things that they believe they need.

So this is all they want. To survive! But let's be real. If all of their friends and families were slaves with them. Who could they go work for? It's not hard to understand.

They can only work for the people that own businesses! Now for real. What's the chances of a slave becoming free tomorrow in automatically having their own business?

They went back to work for the same people who has been helping keep them down.

Also think of this. If the people with farms and businesses were used to have slaves working for free. Why would they want to pay them all of a sudden? I mean think about it yourself. Don't just agree with me.

Why would they want to give any of their money to the same people that they used to force to work for free? The only thing different is that the constitution of America states that slavery shall not exist, unless the person have been convicted of a crime.

So if you don't want to get arrested, you can't have a slave anymore. Owning a business doesn't go against the Constitution. So as an ex-slave owner, of course you don't want to pay your workers, but because the constitution states that you have to, you want to pay them as little as possible!Right? Right?

Of course you would and if you have never been paid for your work, how would you know how much your work is worth? I mean you never got a paycheck or check stub. So how would you know what to expect?

You don't even know what money can do! All you know is what was taught to you! Nothing more.

So guess what they settled for?

Whatever their ex slave Master decided to give them or the bare minimum that the law required them to pay. Why would they give them more than what was required? They wouldn't.

Before, they were slave masters paying them nothing. Now they are the business owners paying them the bare minimum which is required. Trust me. It was only the bare minimum.

Money is money no matter how much. It mattered, but not as much as you would think.

Why would it when you don't even know what it can do for you? All you know is what you want and need! That's it. What was their purpose for working? To purchase food, clothing, and to provide themselves with a place to live! This is what they needed. So this is what they work for.

Now think about it for yourself. What kind of food could they afford? What kind of clothes could they afford? What kind of home could they afford? That's right. Whatever you can afford with the bare minimum!

But don't stop thinking there. Keep going because you are beginning to understand the cycle.

If they never received true education. Did they know how to budget their bare minimum? Of course not. Most of them bought what they wanted and needed today. Then tomorrow had nothing! They never enjoyed money so they didn't understand how to use it or save it for that matter.

How could they? They only knew what they knew. They knew that they were hungry today. So what would they have thought was the smartest thing to do in their shoes? Buy food today. Right?

Okay. That's what they did. Now tomorrow is something that would just have to be thought about tomorrow. On the bare minimum pay wages you can't expect to have everything, but let's just be real. I mean as real as possible.

When you work your whole life and receive everything that you need for free. What else do you assume you need? What else do you want? Nothing. Right?

So now that you have to work and pay for your own lifestyle, what do you spend your money on? You don't just think of things that you don't know about. You think of what you want and need!

When you have children, what do you teach them to work for? What they want and need! Nothing more and nothing less.

Now fast-forward decade, after decade, after the decade. Jobs get better. Laws change. The bare minimum wage grows, but what you want and need does not change.

You only learn what is taught! What was taught to your parents they will teach to you. Decade, after decade, after decade. This is "why we're broke and they're rich."

Chapter 3

What's our problem?

Flipping through the pages of "history" is always an emotional thing. It's like reopening wounds that may not have all been completely healed. But not a physical wound on your leg. The mental one that will never truly leave.

The past is like the law enforcer for the future. What happened in a person's past will dictate what their future will be like. When we as a people acknowledge our families prior position in the human structure. We allow ourselves to slightly become in control of our positioning.

We no longer are held as "field negroes." Society has loosened up enough for us to slip through the cracks in the American pavement. Yes, the world is still run by the same families. Yes we are still at the bottom of the food chain, but there are a few of us that have risen to a higher level.

In the American structure we make up the majority at the very bottom. There are plenty of people who have climbed their way up, but still most of us haven't. The American human structure layout mainly goes according to the career path one has chosen.

Starting at the top, going all the way to the bottom. It goes as such. Upper class, middle class, and lower class. The least amount of people being at the very top and more people at the very bottom.

The upper class are the humans that are praised in this society. They are the ones who have everything! It gets no better than them in this country. They are the politicians, celebrities, athletes, doctors, judges, business owners, etc.

Pretty much the famous people amongst their community. Meanwhile their opposite parties are at the bottom of the bottom. No disrespect to anyone reading this, but the people of the lower class are living in poverty.

Bad living conditions come with living in poverty. High crime rates and drug addictions rule those types of areas. People are forced to live in run-down homes and apartments around some of the most ruthless criminals in society.

Rent is fairly cheap. Almost anyone with nothing can survive in this type of living environment. A lot of the people living in lower class are unemployed and for those who have jobs, they work for the bare minimum.

I mean what else would you pay the children of slaves?

Minimum wage is the correct terminology in the 21st century. They receive such a shortage of pay that all they can do is pay for what they want and need! Similar to their ancestors! The one thing that they have in common is their DNA.

They are the descendants of those same slaves that were once set free. They only know what was taught to them. Now let's be real with one another. Before I ask you this question. I want you to understand that in no way am I promoting violence.

I am not trying to create friction between any group of people. What I am doing is educating "my people!" There's nothing wrong with me knowing the truth, nor is it anything wrong with me acknowledging the truth. If anyone tries to say that I am a racist for being honest then they themselves are in denial. If I am wrong I will personally step up to acknowledge my faults, but will you!

Okay! I want you to open your mind and think for yourself. Don't just agree with me. Use your own brain, okay?

Did slavery really exist in America?
If it did, was it okay with the political parties here?
Did the president allow it? What about the police?

So let me ask you this. How did the teachers and principals feel about having to allow black children in their schools after slavery was over? How did the teachers respond to those ex-slaves? Matter of fact, who is in control of the school systems in America?

So after analyzing these questions. It should be obvious that the American school system is ran by the very same families whom at one time had their own slaves or allowed the people to have their own slaves!

Come on now. Picture America having slaves for hundreds of years, but the president, police, military, politicians, doctors, lawyers, and teachers in America disagreeing with it!

I want you to do the math for me. All you have to do is add the pieces together and you will be able to understand why "we" are uneducated about a lot of things. We have been attending their schools!

They teach us what they want us to know! We as a community don't get to choose the daily curriculums that are taught in school. We as parents have no say so. "We" just send our children to "their" schools to learn what they want to teach them!

Of course some people are going to dispute this but I don't care. Not because I'm rude. Not because I'm disrespectful. Not because I'm racist, but because I am speaking the truth!

Our children only know what we teach them and what they teach them. The most important subject in a fast-growing society like America is math! Why is there no curriculum on the subject we call "money"? Why are schools not teaching children the value of a dollar? Why aren't there any investment classes in elementary school? Why aren't our children learning how to own businesses? This is "why we're broke and they're rich."

We only know what we are taught from our family, community, and schools! We obviously can't teach each other about business ownership because most of us don't own any, but they do. So while they are teaching their children to start businesses and how to invest their money. We are teaching ours how to work for the bare minimum and to buy what they need.

What's more crazy about it is that we aren't teaching our children to buy cheap clothing and belongings. We influence them to spend their bare minimum incorrectly! Come on now. We all know that lower-class citizens tend to buy the most expensive things.

The most expensive clothes, cars, and even the most expensive hairstyles. Let's keep it real. How crazy are we? First of all we settle for the worst paying jobs. Then we have the nerve to spend our bare minimum wages on expensive name brand clothing!

We are not taking our money seriously. We are working hard just to pay for food, clothing, and housing, but what kind of food can we afford with the bare minimum wages?

What kind of clothes can we afford with the bare minimum wages?

What kind of housing can we afford with the bare minimum wages?

The bare minimum!

We are just continuing the exact same behaviors as our families did hundreds of years ago. We are still showing the same mentality of our slave ancestors! I've heard it time and time again the stupid comments of my people. "As long as my bills are paid I'm happy!" That is not the way to live. All that means is that you are only working to provide food, clothing, and shelter. What is the difference between us and our slave ancestors?

Do you think you're better than them because you aren't being whipped? You can't tell that you are doing the same exact thing that they were! Where do you work? How much do you get paid? How much do you get paid per hour?

Now think about it. How many hours did you work this week in order to pay for those shoes that you have on your feet? Are those name brand clothes that important?

What about owning a business? Why don't you invest your money in something long-term? It's time for a change! Am I saying something wrong or am I telling the truth?

Why do we settle for the bare minimum then spend it on expensive clothing? Why do we settle for the bare minimum only to spend it on surviving? Why do we allow the same system that has abused and enslaved our people to teach our children? This is "why we're broke and they're rich!"

Chapter 4

How do we correct our problem?

We fight! We fight! We fight! Not each other physically like we have been doing. Not people outside of our race because of the past. Our own crab in the barrel mentality. Our own degrading moral and value system. The moral and value system that "they" continue to give us.

Our community. Our culture. Lower class. Even middle-class. We are a reflection of a broken mirror used to cover up our vision. We walk around our filthy neighborhood like it is a palace!

Why do we accept that kind of environment for our children? I know a few people that live the "American dream." They all have nice homes, nice cars, and beautiful children. Even the little businesses on the corner of the projects. I'll be honest, they're doing okay for themselves.

Almost everyone in their family is either in college or a college graduate. I remember having a couple of conversations with a gentleman that is the head of his household.

I asked him how he became so successful. He got a little talkative immediately talking for hours. He went from one topic to another. I'm not going to lie to you though. I took in a lot of the information.

He spoke so much that I couldn't repeat the entire conversation. The only thing that is worth explaining at this moment was the end of his mini speech. "I figured out the system." He said. "I thought of how Americans have been prospering and I found myself. Instead of living like a minority from another country. I decided to live like an American."

Now for most people those statements might not have been useful. Hopefully it is not that difficult for you to read in between the lines, but even if it was I am here to help you. This was the most valuable piece of his message to me because he identified his roots before anything.

I'm not saying that we as a people should dislike America. I'm not suggesting that we should act like we weren't born in this country. What I am saying is that we need to at least acknowledge the root of ourselves and this country. Before we can live the correct way in this country, we need to look at it like we are outsiders. Because we are!

This is why foreigners come here and achieve more than us! We were born in the American human structure and they weren't. So it is easy for them to identify what position they want to have in it.

When you can view the winners and losers of a society. You get a chance to evaluate their situations that led up to their success or failure. This allows you to take the appropriate steps to accomplish whatever you want.

This is why I truly value the conversation between my friend and I. He made me look at things differently. The way he spoke about his success showed me another light in this darkness called America!

For years "we" have accepted the position that was given to us in this human structure. We have been so blind to reality that we don't even see the whole structure!

Look at the top. Why are we not trying to reach it? They do. So when will "we" begin to realize where "we" are? This is America! The successful people in this country all do the same things. Remember the American human structure layout is as follows. Upper class, middle class, and lower class.

How about we stop being content with our position and try to rise to a better class. If we take a look at the difference between lower class citizens and upper class citizens, we can start to understand a lot better. What separates us? Of course. MONEY!

They are millionaires and we are making the bare minimum. They go to college and we barely finish high school. They owned businesses, while we work for their business! They continue to do better while we continue to do worse.

When you evaluate them, you see their consistency to do better. They understand money! They seem to know what money should be used for. Now I'm not saying that "we" are dumb. I'm just saying that we are not thinking hard enough.

We should be forcing ourselves to strive for a better life! We should communicate with people that are doing better. Let me ask you this and I want you to be honest with yourself. Okay?

What is wrong with being rich? For real! What is wrong with being rich? Why don't we strive for it? I know that it is clear that the people that go to college can get a better job than those who don't. So why don't we get together to make sure that these beautiful children in our community go to college?

"We" all know that lower class sucks. We all are tired of being "broke". So let's start thinking like Americans! How many of you know about politics? Come on, be real.

Who knows about economics? How many of you have friends and family members close to you that know about currency?

Okay. Now let's get this understood. I'm not trying to bash anyone. I don't want to hurt anyone's feelings. I just want you to be real and see why there are so many of us at the bottom of the human structure. We haven't been taught anything, but it was designed like that.

It's been like that and we are still blaming everyone else because we have not all overcome. Now it is time to check ourselves! We have to look at our problems in order to understand how to place ourselves in a better position in the human structure.

Why are we not trying! They try to get an education. Even if it isn't what they want. They might not enjoy school. They might think that it is boring. It doesn't matter though. Why? Because they are doing what it takes in order for them to live the kind of lifestyle that they want.

This is our major problem. We don't know what kind of lifestyle we want! We view the only lifestyle that we know with a glamorous eye lens. We think that because we have a place to stay, that we are better than the people without one.

We look at the people with no name brand shoes and laugh because we have on Jordan's. We act like we are somebody because we got back a couple of thousand dollars on our tax return!

This isn't life though. We are at the bottom of the human structure. We should start communicating with each other in a better manner. We all need motivation. When we start to educate ourselves on the problems of our people. We start to overcome.

There are positions hiring for doctors and nurses all the time. The only thing about it is that you can't get one of those jobs without the proper education. There are plenty of powerful black people in the world that started at the bottom.

They would love to help us, but how can they help us if we never put ourselves around him! Friendships and connections are important when it comes to success. All successful people know successful people. They live amongst one another in upper-class communities.

Find some and ask them how they made it to be where they are. If you or someone you know wants to be a lawyer. It would be smart to go to a law firm and speak with a real lawyer. Ask them what they had to do to become a lawyer.

One thing that you'll learn from talking to successful people is that they love talking about their success! Don't be afraid to speak about what you want. Even around your friends and families. Talk to them about what you want, so they can add to the positive conversation.

In order to continue growth we have to start working on growing! Once we think about how we want to live, we can start to make the proper adjustments in our lives.

The bad habits of today play a big part in the failure of tomorrow! Understanding finances and success is the first step to success. Look at it from the outsiders perspective.

What is the difference between what lower-class citizens do and what upper-class citizens do? What kind of jobs do they have in upper-class communities? What kind of jobs do they have in lower-class communities? Now research it.

Think about it. Talk about it. Do whatever you have to do! Learn how to qualify for these jobs. Teach your children what to do! Teach your children what they teach their children. Put your children in the same schools that they put their children in.

Give your children a chance to succeed. If you see what they see, then you'll know what they know! Take your children to their parks. Let them have a chance at making good friendships and connections while they're young.

Keep them influenced by the type of things that upper-class children are influenced by. Make them go to school! They don't necessarily have to enjoy it. Just make sure they understand what a good education can do for them.

Teach them about money and investing. This is the only way to get them ready for adulthood. Before we just threw our children into the fast-paced American society. We need to prepare them for it! The worst thing that "we " do to our children is let them learn on their own.

I hear people say things like, "she'll learn the easy way or the hard way." Or "he'll have to learn one way or another." This sucks! Our children did not create themselves. There's no reason why they should have to raise themselves! There is definitely no reason why they need to learn on their own!

We have to make sure that they are ready because when it is time for them to become an adult, we can't reverse time. When it is time, it is time. Think about it. For real! When a child grows up, who buys them what they need? Who feeds them? Who do they live with? Their parents right? Okay.

At 2 years old you don't get up and work for yourself. You don't invest in stocks and bonds. You don't know the value of money! All you know is that when you go to the store with your parents you want candy.

Sometimes the parents get it and sometimes their parents don't. When they can't get it, what do the parents say? "Baby not today, I don't have any money for that right now."

This is a child's first understanding of money. It can buy candy. As you get older your wants start to change. It starts to be toys, games, clothes, and etc. No matter what it is, you go to your parents for it. Why? Because you don't have money of course.

Now later on when you become an adult you get a job. What do you buy? Things that you want, that were once free to you. Maybe things that you feel as though you didn't receive as a kid.

Things that you can get now that you're grown. Why? Because this is what money can do. Buy you things that you want and need. This is what most of us do. We understand money because of how it was explained to us!

Come on, be serious right now. How many of us heard our parents say. "Hold on baby I have to invest this money before I buy you those shoes"? But I'm pretty sure you heard, "hold on baby I have to go to work, then when I get paid I'll buy those shoes."

Imagine if your parents' excuse was always because they had to invest their money first. You would have learned that same thing. Then when you started to get your own money your first thought would be to invest it before you spend it.

You only know what is taught to you! For now, "we" as a people need to enter the beginning stage. This stage is not a physical thing. It is a mental one. We need to start learning what money is and how it can work for us.

What is money for? It's not what we have been using it for. We as a people of the 21st century have so many opportunities to move up, but we are not taking advantage of it.

Money is way more powerful than what you know. We are way more powerful than what we know. Before we can teach our children how powerful they are, shouldn't we know first?

Come on now. We cannot teach our children things that we don't know about. We as parents and adults in our community need to stand up. We need to become leaders.

If we don't come together and learn we can't come together and teach! Support is the key. If I have your support, my word becomes more powerful. If you support me, I have more people in my corner. The more intellectual people we have in our corner, the more people we have that can think about how to overcome.

Misguidance and miseducation shall no longer be the reason "why we're broke and they're rich."

Chapter 5

What is support?

It's about time we start standing together. It's been a long time since we have seen our good old friend "loyalty"! Do you know how many times I've been in public places like the mall or School. Even places like the park. I see unity outside of my own community. Unity inside there's.

It's kind of crazy when you ask me. I'm just being real. Just last week I was at Piedmont Park in Atlanta Georgia. I was walking with my headphones on. You know, just listening to my music when I noticed a mom and her two children. A little boy and a little girl.

They were playing with a Frisbee. Now, I wasn't trying to stare at them but they did catch my eye for a second. It was nice seeing them play together when all of a sudden another family comes over. First the parents started speaking to each other and then the children started playing.

Nothing out of the ordinary, right? I begin to jog around the park alone. Just relaxing my mind. I might have ran about 8 laps before I stopped. I noticed how the park had grown from one lady and two children to about 12 parents and 20 children.

They were all having such a great time. It was kind of weird that all of these people just came over to play. So I asked the next group of people walking over. "Exactly what is going on?" They told me that they didn't even know. They said that they saw a sign in the front of the park and just decided to come over.

So here I am all nosy. I went over to the front of the park to see what sign they were speaking of and there it was. A sign that said. "Hey it's Hector's 7th birthday. Our family is back in Mexico so help us celebrate. Please!" I laughed because it was just crazy to me that all of these people didn't even know each other, but they still went over there.

I had never seen anything like it. I went home puzzled. I couldn't believe that someone would put up a stupid sign like that and people would actually come. It was so great that it made me mad.

Now I'm not saying that I was mad because I was jealous of them. I'm not a hater or anything, but to be honest I was a little jealous! I'm happy that they were having fun. I really am. I'm happy that little Hector could enjoy his birthday, but I was mad because I couldn't imagine anyone joining my son for his birthday if I had put up that same exact sign.

Come on man! I could hear my people now. "Oh no! I'm not going to let you play with those bad kids. What's wrong with them that they have to beg people to come to their party."

I mean correct me if I'm wrong. We have got to be the most judgmental people ever. I don't know what it is about us, but we hate seeing each other do well. Matter of fact that's a lie. I do know what is wrong with us! We are doing so bad that we can't stand to see others doing good.

If I would have put up that same sign it would have been so many people watching from a distance. Hoping that no one would come over just so that they could laugh.

Do you want to know another reason "why we're broke and they're rich." They have a great support system! They are each other's support system. When someone is attempting to do good in their community. They receive help from one another. "If you scratch my back I'll scratch yours." That's what they say.

A favor for a favor. It is the complete opposite in our community. We as a people of the lower class seem to pull each other down. When we see people doing well there are a lot of us that speak wrongly about them.

The smart people in our neighborhood get picked on and called nerds. The pretty women speak down on each other to hurt each other self esteem. On another note. When some people see others getting money and enjoying life, they want to hurt or rob them.

We have no one to go to for motivation. Even when someone in our community gets a job. There are always people that will have something negative to say. "Oh so you think you're doing something because you got a job." Or "look at him acting all brand new since he got that job."

For real. We are seriously our own haters. What we do to ourselves, they don't have to do! Just think about it. When someone is trying to open a business. Wouldn't it be easy for other business owners to teach them what to do?

How hard is it to show a newcomer what you had to do to become successful? It can't be hard. It should actually be very easy to talk about yourself. They don't have a problem spreading the wealth.

To them they look at it as if it's better to help their neighbor be a better neighbor. This is what we lack. Why don't we help each other do better? If there is a family-owned business in our community wouldn't it be easy to go to them for advice about business ownership?

We don't even allow others to shine. We look at each other as if they are hurting us rather than helping. What we as lower class citizens need to realize is that support is a good thing to have. If we would just understand what they understand we would be way better off.

They know how to bring money into their community. They understand the karma behind supporting one another. We obviously don't. We think "why should I help him get rich," but we don't understand that we are helping people in other communities instead of helping the ones in ours!

If we help just one family from our community establish themselves. They can help us! They'll generate enough income to the point where they will need more space. If they want more space they will need more workers.

This will in fact increase the opportunity for more people in the community to have a job. Also this gives more future entrepreneurs in the community chances to network and rub shoulders with business owners.

The more help our own people receive with their business. The more jobs they will create! The more money we have the better! But instead of helping each other, we continue to help them! We buy their overpriced food. We buy their overpriced clothing. Only to become broker!

Just for them to become richer. Why don't we start our own clothing lines? Our own fashion that we all agree with. That way everyone can afford it and the money stays in our community. Better yet, why don't the people in the community come together to create their own economic system?

Seriously! We all might not have the best jobs, but if we all come together with our money it will add up! We could start off small with our own transportation service. This can allow us to have a way to get to work. Our kids won't have to walk to school. No more cabs on Sunday after church. Anything will help. We have to stop being our own worst enemy.

If we claim to love our neighborhood so much we need to take care of it and help build it. Let's start coming together to support the college students.

Let's make sure they have food and clothing so they don't have to struggle while they're in school! The more college graduates in the neighborhood the more people there will be that actually have an opportunity to get a decent career.

Just think about it. If we all support each other the right way. Help one another get through college. The more money we can make and keep amongst ourselves. This would then make us all qualify to become business partners!

This would definitely be the ultimate reason for the rise of "our" people. Lower class citizens would no longer exist if we all acknowledge and fix what is keeping us in the lower class position.

Scratch my back so I can scratch yours. Let's open up a few businesses so our children can have jobs! Who do you think their children work for? For their parents. Definitely not ours!

How about supporting the man next to you and stop supporting the man you will probably never meet! Help a family that will help your family. Help a family that lives in your community.

We need to get it into our skulls.we need each other! The more people who climb up the human structure from our neighborhood, the more people we have to help us make it up.

Why do you think it's so easy for them to do good? What, do you think they do it on their own? Of course not! First off, their parents teach and help them. Then their friends help them.

They are always their own support system. Now that I'm thinking about it. Let me address something else. Don't feel offended all right? Why do "we" make our children move out so soon? Why do we make our kids get their own before they are truly ready?

I've noticed this so often. We make our children get jobs at 18 so they can get their own apartments at a young age. Then if they don't have their own, we make them feel so awkward in our home!

Not to be racist or anything but Mexicans don't do that. They don't mind their children living with them until they are ready to go. No matter how small the apartment either. There can be 7 adults and 5 children in a three-bedroom apartment. They don't care. Why? Because all seven adults have a job.

They may even all work at the same place, so they might only have one car. This makes it easier on them because there are 7 people chipping in on bills. 7 people that can help feed those children.

7 people that can help start a business. This sure beats the one mom in our house that has to pay all of the bills on her own! Buy and cook food on her own! This is why "we" as a community continue to do bad. Each one of our individual homes consists of only one or two incomes. Bare minimum income at that.

If we stayed unified with one another and didn't make our family uncomfortable in our house we would have a better living condition. The more incomes the better. Forget independence. What we need in our community is help! Forget dependency. What we need in our community is a better support system! We lack a good support system. "This is why we're broke and they're rich."

Chapter 6

Stop being content!

What's right is right. What's wrong is wrong. What's true is true. What's false is false. Can we agree on that? If I told you that the sky is blue, could we agree on that? I hope so.

Living in America has been what it has been. I did not make my life. Neither did you for that matter. Our parents are who we should give thanks to. If it wasn't for our parents we would not have been born. I appreciate my mother and father for coming together and creating me.

They tried their best to give me a good life. I'm not going to lie and say that it was perfect or anything, but I will say that they tried. I had the basic things like clothing, food and a place to live.

We never went on any adventures. Nice vacations or anything that I see happy families do on TV. We just lived in poverty. So did the rest of my family. We all live in the same crime infested neighborhoods. To be real. I loved to hear the sounds of police sirens and gunshots.

I mean I was only a kid and to all of my friends that lifestyle was cool. We watched the same things on BET and it was glorified in the rap music that we listen to.

To us, we were living the hood life. It has always been put to us in a cool way. So that's the way we perceive it. For real. Just think about it. All of the cool rappers that we listen to talk about drugs, sex, and guns.

All of the movies that we watched showed drugs, sex, and guns. We were living like rappers and movie stars.

That is what made us love living in the ghetto. It seemed as if it was the only place that was cool to live.

When I got a little older. I started to behave just like the rappers and actors on the TV. I mean why not? They seem to make a lot of money doing what they were doing, so why shouldn't I?

It just was so cool to me. I began to be content with living in the lower class. All of my friends were too. Together we were the Boys in the Hood. To Newark New Jersey boys. That's what we were. Until I moved to Georgia.

When I moved to Georgia I started to see a different type of living. A different type of person. I began to see houses that I would have never thought existed. Cars that only rich people had. The type of living conditions that made me feel safe. For the first time in my life I felt safe!

It's crazy now when I think about it. How can I feel comfortable in a stranger's community but I feel on my guard in my own? The longer I stayed in Georgia, the nicer things seemed to be. The nicer the people began to be.

I went from being in a crime infested neighborhood to the quiet suburbs. My friends even changed. I started with friends that rob, steal, and commit crimes to get money. Then ended up with friends who work and owned businesses to earn their money.

To be honest. I even feel more comfortable around my new friends. I know that they don't steal so I'm not scared to bring them in my house. The older I get, the happier I am with my new living conditions. I'm so happy with my new living conditions that I hate my old ones.

I hate the way I used to live! Those friends that I had back home in New Jersey still live the same way. I don't even enjoy the same types of music anymore nor do I enjoy the same movies. I see it as glorifying a lifestyle of hatred!

I barely even visit my old neighborhood anymore. Things just haven't changed. Now don't get me wrong, I'm not saying anything wrong about anyone. Like I said. " I did not make my life. Neither did you for that matter. Our parents are who we should give thanks to."

Which means I understand that if a parent gives birth to a child in a crime infested neighborhood, then it would be raised in a crime infested neighborhood! It's not our fault where we lived as a kid.

I know that just like everyone else does. I just don't understand how we as a people can get content with such a horrible lifestyle. If we don't look at our situation and be real with ourselves about it we will never understand the truth about ourselves.

We are born innocent children. We as innocent children have nothing to do with what is being glorified in the entertainment business, but for some reason innocent children get sucked into this bad stigma that is set upon "our" people. This is what makes us content with these bad living conditions because it seems like this lifestyle is the correct way to live.

We watch the bull crap on the television that is given to our community. We listen to the bull crap music on the radio that is given to our culture. So we in return live the way that is designed for us to live.

We are so blind to life itself, that we think that this is all life has to offer. Never mind peace, love, and happiness. We are content with drugs, sex, and guns! We live in a society that has fed us so much poison that we forget how to eat healthy.

A fun day for "our" people is chilling in the neighborhood on the corner listening to sirens and gunshots. A fun day for "our" people is hanging on the block!

The same block that is crime, drug, and gang-infested! How do we fall victim and become content with a bullshit lifestyle? None of our people even think about changing the channel to watch the inspiring lifestyle of the rich.

In order for "us" to become rich or to even change we have to give up the behaviors of the past. For years and years, we have been living horribly. For years and years, we have been content with being lower class citizens!

When we decide that we want to move up in the human structure of America we can put together the appropriate steps to climb up. But until "we" stop accepting this crappy lifestyle, "we" will never be able to guarantee our children a better life.

For 1. Stop accepting the bare minimum wages! I don't want to hear "that's all I can do!" I truly don't because that is not the truth. you can do a whole lot more than the bare minimum! All you have to do is try.

If you are grown and don't have the experience that the better position requires. You need to get some type of training on your side. There are tons of vocational training skills, trade skills, or even online classes that can be taken up. I don't want to hear, " I'm too old for that." You're never too old to make something better for yourself.

That's another one of the problems my people have. "We" have. We always deprive ourselves of the better things. As people of the 21st century we need to notice the opportunities that are available to us. We have the privileges that our family before us did not have!

School is for everyone. The internet is for everyone. Today we have a lot of things that we can utilize to improve our life, but why does our Google search only show porn?

Why does our Google search only have trending topics on it? Why does it only have gossip about celebrities? We all have the opportunity to learn anything with the technology of today. We use it to learn nothing! It seems to me that we have a bigger issue in life.

The way we hinder ourselves and each other from becoming successful, it appears to be fear! We must be scared of success! We have to be! I'm not convinced why, but it seems as if fear is stopping us from reaching our full potential.

The way we reject success and positivity is ridiculous. There is no reason why we should continue to hold on to the belief system of a broken society! We as lower class citizens have no room to point our fingers at anyone doing good saying. " I'm doing better than you." We are all broke!

We should be working hard to build our bank account. We should be working hard to build our credit score. We should be working hard for our own businesses! Why are there so many of us who have goals and still don't chase them? I'm talking for real.

I know so many people in my community that love to play baseball, basketball, and football for that matter. Guess what though? They are better than a lot of the rich athletes on TV. They get props for their ability everywhere in the community. They even bet each other on games. Then when it's time to go to school. They don't even play!

They let their talent go to waste. Why? Because they don't want to miss the next gang meeting. The next live Street episode of who's on the block, but what is even worse than them wasting their talent is that the parents let them do it!

Instead of pushing them to the limit. Showing them how sports can be the way up the human structure. They let their children make the biggest mistakes of their life. Wasted talent. This is what my community, I mean "our " community is filled with.

There are so many beautiful, beautiful little girls that have the potential to be models. All they need is guidance from their parents and they can do it. If not models. They could be actresses, singers, songwriters, or the first female president! But instead of their families making it their duty to make sure these girls do something powerful. They let them do what "they " want them to do.

Now when those same exact women are older look at them. On section 8! Four children! Three baby daddies! Broke! Some even alcoholics or drug addicts. Yes, weed is a drug!

Come on now, "my" people. We need To do better than this. We need to want more than this, we need to want more for our children! Why don't we? Truthfully. Be honest. Are "our" people scared of success? Be real. Are "our" people scared of money? Or am I the only one that sees the consistent, lazy, scary tendencies of "our" people.

For years and years we had to struggle just to fall victim to the unhappiness of the ghetto later on. The urban community. We lack ambition. Most of us lack education. We lack morals and values. We lack the understanding of happiness.

It is now our fault for holding our position at the bottom of the human structure. Of course we can blame it on the music. " Well it's not my fault. The music is so negative that it makes us negative."

We can say that, but is that the whole truth? Of course it's not. Why? Because we choose to keep listening to it! If we start to listen to inspirational music, then we can overcome the negative influence.

If we start to watch positive inspirational movies then we can enjoy the education and positive influence of it. But as long as we continue to let them feed our children that bull crap entertainment they will continue to be influenced by it.

Think about it. If you continue to say mommy in front of your baby. What will they say? Mommy, right? If you always feed them oatmeal. What will they ask for when they get hungry? Oatmeal, right?

Okay then, so what do you think they'll do when they constantly hear this gangsta music? What will they become? Gangsters, right? Come on "my " people it is common sense that "our" children are not being influenced with positivity! It's obvious that they are being fed bullcrap!

When will we stop being content with this bull crap! Until we stop being content with this bullcrap lifestyle. This will continue to be one of the reasons `` why we're broke and they're rich!"

Chapter 7

What they know!

Focus. Focus your mind on the world. Think of the trees and clouds. Think of a waterfall. Oh! Look at the group of dolphins jumping out of the water. Are they beautiful or what? Relax yourself enough to let your brain run free. In and out.

Now think about yesterday.
Think about what you did when you woke up. Did you have a smile on your face or were you mad! Did you have a bad dream or was it a good one? What did you eat for breakfast, lunch, and dinner?

Fast forward to today? When you woke up. Be real. How much money did you wake up with? I'm not just talking about in your pockets. I'm talking about all together. Your pockets, your stash, your bank, and wherever else you put money.

Is it the same amount that you woke up with yesterday? How about 2 days ago? If you go all the way back to last Friday. Would you say you have more money now or less? Come on now. Think about it.

Has your money been growing day by day or does it decrease? Focus just a little bit longer. If you can. I want you to think back to the same exact day last year. How much money would you say you had? Of course, thinking back that far could be hard, but if you could just do it. Did you?

If you really did it then you'll understand what "they" understand. Money is meant to be traded for things with the same or greater value. If you don't trade it, you should save it. The purpose of making money is not to spend it all as soon as you get it. It is to be utilized only when it is needed.

The times of need or the times of need. No one can tell you when you will need something. Things just happened. Good and bad things happen unexpectedly. In the 21st century we live by a system.

Currency is the baseline of every system, so in our times of need. We need currency! A big problem in my community, excuse me. A big problem in "our" community is financial stability.

" We" as a people have not been taught financial stability. "We" all have been taught how to work. We all have been taught how to get a few dollars, but we all haven't been taught what to do with money after we get it!

Of course, if you don't teach someone what to do with money they will not fully understand what to do with money. This is common sense. The only thing they will do with it is what they know, what was taught, or they will come up with their own.

A lot of us have great teachers in life, not just in school but at home. A lot of us have been taught about savings and checking accounts. A lot of us may have been taught about credit cards.

Most of us have no clue about these things though! all of lower class has the same problem. It's money! None of us use money to its full potential. it's easy to get defensive and say that you do, but you wouldn't be a lower-class citizen if you did! " We" all use money wrongly. "We" all need to be re-educated about the purpose of money. Yes, money can and does pay bills. Yes, money can and does feed our children. But it also doesn't have to be spent! It can be placed in a bank and the amount can grow. It can be used to start a business. It can be used to invest in stocks, bonds, and mutual funds. It can *also be used to fund programs to help the community, invest in new ideas, and inventions.*

Money shouldn't always be spent as soon as we get it but that is exactly what we as lower-class citizens do. I know so many people that live paycheck-to-paycheck. These people have decent jobs. More than minimum wage, but still not enough to be considered above lower class.

They pile so much on their shoulders. I mean I'm not knocking them because I do respect the fact that they provide for their families. I'm just saying that I see their problem. They simply have put themselves on a steady responsibility level.

No more, no less, but steady. They have decent living conditions for their children. Decent cars to drive. Nice accessories for their home. They are comfortable, but every month they always say that they are broke.

They get paid two to three times a month. Every month, but they always have the same excuse. The rent, light bill, car insurance, car note, food, and etc. They have accumulated so many bills that even though they make a decent amount of money they don't ever have any money left after they pay them. Most of the time they can't even afford to go out and enjoy themselves with their friends. So all they do is work and go home.

After having their jobs for about a year or so I find them all looking like they are moving up. Newer cars. Nice jewelry. Better clothes. I'm not going to lie. They keep themselves looking nice everywhere they go, but for some reason whenever something goes wrong. You know those unexpected things like engine problems, family members needing financial assistance, or even valuable belongings getting damaged. It always seems to really set them back for a while. But here's why.

They have adjusted their financial responsibilities according to how much money they make at their jobs. Knowing how much they will receive has made them feel as though they can make their bills a little more expensive.

For example, they may have started with a pay rate of $1,000 every two weeks. So they figured that it was okay to lease a car because they could afford the $300 a month car note. They also decided to rent a nice apartment where the water is not free, so that became an extra bill. Along with their car insurance and other living expenses. This led to them having to dish out a total of $800 every two weeks.

Not including their daily spending habits on food, clothing, and miscellaneous things. Now what's bad about this is they have put themselves in a tight financial hold. Which means they have no room for anything else except for planned expenses. Anything unexpected will hurt them severely.

Not including a missed day at work. Oh man! That could be the reason that their lights get cut off. But what's worse about it is. When they do get a little extra money from doing overtime or a pay increase. They start to add more bills to their load. 10 hours overtime! Now they decide to release the new iPhone. A 50 cent raise! Now it's time to get the new cable service.

Every time they get a little more money they just start giving it away! Now trust me I am not trying to bash anyone, so I'm not going to say any names. But what I will say is that they are not the only ones that seem to do this. Most of "our" people do it! The more money we make. The more things we buy.

This is one of the main reasons why we can't help ourselves climb up the human structure. We are too busy trying to spend money, when we need to be saving it. For the most part. None of "our" people have a good sense of what it means to be financially stable.

To "us" it means to have a steady income. For "them" it is something totally different. They understand what we don't. Money makes money. Before money is spent on anything it could be invested. It should be invested! Investments are opportunities to grow your financial situation. "They" understand the purpose of money.

With that understanding comes budgeting. Something that most of "us" don't seem to actually know how to do. Budgeting is one of the key elements to gaining wealth.

"They" might work the same job as "us", with the same pay and overtime. The difference between "them" and "us"will show in their daily spending habits.

The things that are not needed like fast food, drugs, alcohol, and etcetera will not be purchased daily. They're clothes. Oh my God! Their clothes won't cost anywhere near as much as ours! I know a lot of people might say, " well what about the Gucci, Fendi, and the Prada." Those are very expensive clothing. I can admit that. But the thing we are not understanding is that those clothes weren't meant for lower class citizens! It was meant for people that could afford to pay $495 on a belt!

That clearly is not in the budget of someone that makes the bare minimum. It was meant for the upper-class citizens. If someone is in our work salary cap, they can't afford it. This is why they save their money. Then they can take advantage of their saved money and invest. Soon "they" would have excelled pass "us" to becoming business owners while we become "swagged out."

How ridiculous our daily spending habits are. When you think about it. I actually mean think about it. You will understand that "we " spend the majority of our hard-earned money in the matter of minutes. Which causes us to remain broke until we work hard for days to receive our next paycheck.

Then because we were broke the entire week or two. We have no choice but to spend our new check to make up for our stressful days. This is our repeated cycle throughout our entire working life! Which makes us depend on every hour of work.

Every hour is needed in order for us to even maintain our crappy lifestyle. The bull crap lifestyle that we as lower class citizens have, takes so much hard work to keep.

While "we" are working hard to maintain that lifestyle that "we" truly don't even want. "They" are working hard to increase "their" investment opportunities! Then later on. While "we" are still working hard to maintain a lifestyle that "we" truly don't even want. "They" are relaxing on vacation watching "their" bank accounts grow because of "their" investments.

What we fail to realize is that we don't need to spend money just because we have it! We are too busy trying to play the catch-up game that we haven't even read the rules. There's no way to claim that you have money if you don't have money! No matter where you work. No matter how much you make. It doesn't matter if you spent it already.

"My" people have so many problems within themselves that they cannot figure out which one is stopping them from becoming successful. I watched my people drag each other down with their foolish mindset. We always feel like we have to be better than the next person.

If we can't be better than someone else. We will try to look better. You know how "we" do! If the next door neighbor leases the new charger. We go at lease the new Cadillac. When our children see their friends with the new Nikes. They want the new Jordan's.

"We" are in so much competition with each other that "we" are the reason that "we" all fail. Why do we even want that flashy car anyway? That doesn't even look right. Pulling up with this nice expensive clean car to the filthy apartments that we live in!

The nasty crack infested neighborhood. The loud blocks that are run by the Bloods and Crips! I'm just being real. "My" people should not be trying to show off or be flashy in front of people that don't have anything.

They don't mind taking things because they don't have anything to lose! Come on now let's be serious. I'm not going to sugarcoat it. "My" people are ruining their own lives with these foolish ways. What we do to ourselves, they don't have to do!

I love myself enough to extend my hand to my brothers and sisters. "We" need to develop another moral and value system. The one that we have is not going to make us happy. The one that we have is designed to keep us at the bottom!

Why do we continue to do what is not working? We don't acknowledge our failure as failure! For some reason it appears as if we view our failure as if it is success. Living in poverty is the result of failure! Living in the lower class is considered to be a failure! Not being able to help our children go to college is the result of failure!

What's right is right. What's wrong is wrong. What is true is true. What is false is false. Can we agree on that? Well can we also agree that " keeping up with the Joneses' ' is foolishness? Especially when "we" are already broke.

It makes no sense to me, but I do understand what has happened has happened. "We" have been broken so much mentally and physically.1 that we have not yet thought of our financial problems! I mean at one point in time "we" were not able to make money. So now that we can it is going to take some serious thinking and teaching about what we should do with it!

It's not just going to happen without focusing on it. How can someone change without trying? How can we become rich if we are not aware of why we are broke? It won't happen overnight.

Of course. It won't happen unless we focus. Until we focus on what decisions we have made in the past. We will not be able to understand what financial decisions we should make in the future. School is not going to teach us everything about life. It is just one piece of the puzzle.

Our parents are another. Experience is another. Knowledge is another. "We" need to focus and use all of the pieces necessary to fix the puzzle we call life. It's not an easy puzzle. Especially when you don't have the rules!

This is a minor setback for a people with a brighter future, but until "we" start to understand money and how it should be used. Our lack of knowledge will continue to be the biggest reason "why we're broken they're rich!"

Chapter 8

The uprising of the lower-class!

Triumph. Victory. Revenge. Success. Conquerors. Winners. This is what "we" can scream one day. Excuses have been made for the failure of the past. There are none for the success of the future. "We" are the future! Complaints will be made. There will be a lot of anger, but all-in-all the uprising of the lower class will come.

Just be ready. A new day is here. It is no longer the time where "we" say "we" can't. There is no stopping "my" people from climbing up the human structure. I won't allow it! Violence is not an option. Knowledge is the ultimate power!

We will fight back with our mind. Strength comes from within. My children will learn from me and I hope yours can learn from you. But what will you teach them? Will you give them freedom or bondage? Will you teach them the truth or will you shield them from it with lies? America is a country! Will you teach them how to rule it or how to be ruled by its people?

Nothing will stop the uprising of the lower-class! Not even the citizens of the upper class. We need to understand that it is in our hands and no one else's. We have the same rights and we have the same names! We need to start using it.

Never mind the fear of failure. Never mind the shadows of the past. We have rights and we need to start exercising them. Fix your face and watch me fix my bank account. Fix your mouth to ask me how and I'll tell you. Closed mouths don't get fed.

For years we have starved ourselves. It's about time we eat! Let's feast! I promise you that we can do it. Look at Oprah. She is the example of a lifetime. Look at that beautiful billion dollar Queen or should I say billions of dollars. If she can do it, why can't any of you? Don't continue to count yourself out. You are still in the game. You just need to wake up and understand that you are playing!

Read the rules! If you don't think it's important for yourself. Do it for your children! Do it for your grandchildren! Do it for "our" community! The more people we send up the human structure, the more people they can bring with them.

Our position was given to us, not chosen. The human structure has been around before we were born. We just so happen to be born in the family that is at the bottom. Don't be ashamed of your family, they are your family! If you have been born in a position that you don't agree with. You need to think of a way to better your situation.

We all were born innocent children. We all were born in this world without using our position. We all have options now that we have our freedom. Don't ever let anyone make you believe that we don't. It is a new day. The uprising of the lower class is very possible. Without knowledge there can be no revolution.

Violence is not the way. The only way is to re-educate the people. New teachers must teach new teachings. New lessons must be installed. New programs must be developed. New behaviors are the key to new results! No more bad spending habits. No more keeping up with the Joneses.

We have to understand what we are doing wrong in order to stop and do right. We have to notice our failure in order to stop failing. Come on. Do you want your children to be on section 8? What about in a gang? If not then you have to do something different for them.

Stop being content with this horrible lifestyle that we were given! Of course, it wasn't your fault that you were born in a bad environment. Of course, it wasn't your fault that you were born in poverty, but it is your fault if you remain there forever.

It is your fault if your children grow up in poverty. Who can you blame for being 50 years old on food stamps? Come on! Let's take control of our lives. If not for yourself, think about those children. Think about those grandchildren. Do it for the future generations.

We have to create some type of system for them. I can understand if we cannot create a school system for them, but I will not understand it if we don't try! We need to try to improve. If we can't build an entire school. We can still teach each other in our community. In our homes. We must develop a strong support system for one another.

We are all we got, look around! There aren't any outsiders around. No one comes to our neighborhoods, except for us. Why shouldn't we develop a system amongst ourselves? Let's be real. Wouldn't it be smart if we all work together instead of working alone?

The more people on our side, the more money we have. The more ideas we can come up with. We have to start building good positive friendships and connections. Bond with the one that can help. Show respect to each other. Pay attention to what is around you.

Why should we continue to live like animals among civilized people? Think. Focus. Believe. Trust me we can do it if we put our minds to it. They are always trying to do better. They stick together. Let's look at what they do and copy them. I mean why not? Whatever types of business they own we can own too! Just choose a different name.

We have the same opportunities as them, but if we don't understand that, it's worth nothing. It is time for the uprising of the lower class. Until we look at our past, adjust our future, and acknowledge our powers. These ultimately will always be the reasons "why we're broke and they're rich."

Facebook: Neva Eva
Instagram: NevaEvaRecords

About the author;
Hello, I am Isaiah Donaldson Jr the author of this wonderful book.
I am from Newark New Jersey and at this moment in time of actually writing this book I am 27 years old.
I have two beautiful children Amir and Isabella.
I've been through a lot at this time.
I've been incarcerated.
I am not proud to say it, but I am definitely happy to have learned from each and every one of my mistakes.
We as humans do make mistakes and that's one thing that people have to realize.
It is common to make mistakes.
I've been in relationship after relationship after relationship.
So I definitely know a little bit about them.
I'm a great father and for some that may be hard to believe being in the store I'm young and I am African American.

I took my time writing each and every one of my books in the different phases that I was in at the time of writing them.

I never wanted to go on to my next course in life without writing down my previous one.

So after a horrible relationship with my children's mom.

I decided to write this book to inform my future girlfriend how to keep me!

Just because I am from a bad place and have been incarcerated does not mean that I don't deserve to be loved. It does not mean that I don't know how to treat men.

It does not mean that I am a deadly father.

My past is my past and my future is my future.

I will not use my past as an excuse for my future. I will use it as a learning tool in order to correct my present, and manifest my future.

Other books by Isaiah Donaldson Jr
- How to raise boy to be a man
- The science of doing better
- How to turn a boyfriend into a husband
- Why boys join gangs

.

"It is easier to build strong children than to repair broken men"

Frederick Douglass

Made in the USA
Columbia, SC
04 September 2022